I spy with Rembrandt's eye

DE MEESTERWERKEN

THE MASTERPIECES

This publication was made possible by a grant from the Victor Muller Fund

Petra Kana-Devilee and Robert Uterwijk

I spy with Rembrandt's eye

DE MEESTERWERKEN

THE MASTERPIECES

Welcome to the Rijksmuseum,

My name is Rembrandt Harmenszoon van Rijn,
but you can call me Rembrandt.
This is a portrait I did of myself in 1628,
almost 400 years ago.

What's your name?

Paige ♡ Huck

Nice to meet you.

Shall we walk around the museum together?
After all, two see more than one. If you like, I can tell
you a little about my own paintings, and about the art
of my 17-century colleagues.

We'll have to be careful not to touch any priceless art
works by accident. Will you promise to take care? Good!

Sometimes paintings are away at other museums. Then you
can't see them. If you have questions about these paintings,
you can ask about them at the Information desk.

Artus Quellinus

Tympanum of the town hall of Amsterdam
1648

Take a look at this model, made out of clay.
This is what we call a tympanum.

Artus Quellinus is the famous sculptor from Antwerp
who moved to Amsterdam, just like I did.
At that time, Amsterdam was the trading centre of the world,
and that meant there was a lot of work for artists.
Quellinus was asked to decorate the new town hall with sculptures,
to show how important Amsterdam was in the 17th century.
The building turned out to be so magnificent
that it looked more like a palace.

Lady Amsterdam is sitting in the middle, on the railing of a ship.
The whole world is coming to visit her.

Draw a line to the correct headpiece:

Europe wears	sunbonnet
Africa wears	feather headdress
Asia wears	crown
America wears	turban

Can you draw a line from the four heads to the map of the world?

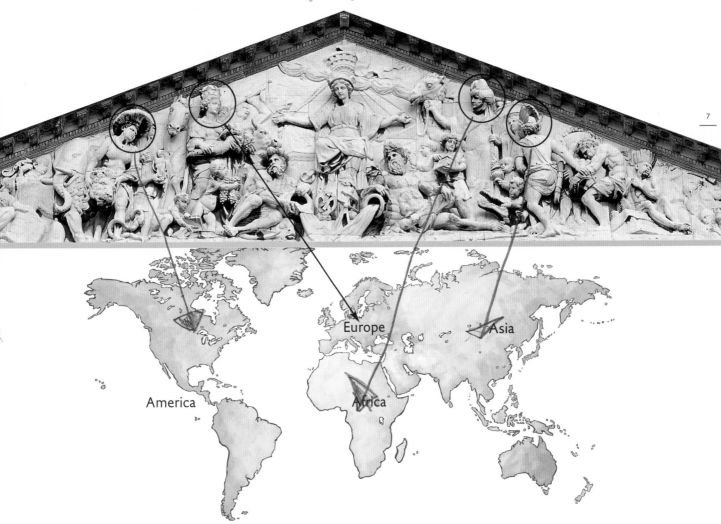

Everyone thought the model was very good. So Artus Quellinus was allowed to make the tympanum in expensive marble. Take your binoculars with you when you go to look at it on the Amsterdam town hall - which is now the Royal Palace - on Dam Square.

Bartholomeus van der Helst

Banquet of the civic guard

1648

This is a festive painting by Bartholomeus van der Helst. Don't the militiamen look splendid? There's so much to see in this painting, maybe you could help me?

How many men do you see without a moustache? ....one...............

How many women can you find?
.................two.................

8

These men – the militiamen – are celebrating. Holland has just signed a peace treaty with Spain.

Put an 'x' next to the glasses used during this celebration.

Not everyone has his own glass, but that doesn't matter. Several people can drink from the same glass. But then they do have to wipe off their greasy mouths beforehand!

The drummer has his serviette on his lap, which is a good thing because he eats with his *fingers.*

Everyone has brought his own knife.

How many knives can you count? *five*

This group portrait was painted by my toughest competitor, Bartholomeus van der Helst. It is very skillfully painted. Do you see the reflection in the captain's breastplate (on the right)?

What's the reflection of?
the men

Frans Post

View of Olinda

1662

*I've never visited any faraway countries myself,
but my colleague Frans Post has been to all sorts of places.
He travelled by ship all the way to Brazil.
His painting - and the frame as well -
are full of all sorts of tropical creatures.*

*Very carefully I copied the animals in the painting
- and the frame - and examined them, one by one.
Aren't they fascinating?*

Can you put them back where they belong by drawing an arrow to the correct place in the painting?

See if you can think up names for all these strange creatures. Write them down next to the pictures.

1 cricket

2 lizard

3 centipede

4 monkey

5 turtle

6 spider

7 armidillo

8 gecko

Petronella Oortman's dolls' house

1686-1710

> This dolls' house is quite magnificent!

Petronella, a very rich lady, had this dolls' house specially made, by a French cabinetmaker.

It's furnished with at least 700 'real' objects. It looks exactly like a grand canal house, but then in miniature. This dolls' house cost Petronella quite a lot of money. She might just have well bought herself a real house on a canal! But for her this was more exciting - and much more fun. Now Petronella could show off her dolls' house and everything inside it to all her friends - and to visitors.

What would it be like to stay in this beautiful house? What would our day look like?

Write the letter of the room under each clock.

16

8 o'clock
We get up. Wasn't that fun, sleeping in a canopy bed?

9 o'clock
Breakfast. Let's have toast in the little kitchen.

10 o'clock
The servant girl is starting on the ironing.

11 o' clock
Visitors who are here to see the master of the house sit down to wait a few minutes.

12 o' clock
Where do you think they've hidden the WC?

1 o'clock
We have tea with Petronella in her room.

2 o'clock
We admire the Chinese porcelain in Petronella's display cabinet.

3 o'clock
Friends of the master are here to look at his collection of shells.

4 o'clock
Time for a game of backgammon in the best parlour.

5 o'clock
There's the doorbell! The coach has come to fetch us. Time to say goodbye.

Adriaen de Vries

Triton

1615-1617

I've never seen this bronze bust by Adriaen de Vries. But I've heard quite a lot about it.
It was <u>part</u> of a huge fountain that stood in the gardens of the king of Denmark.

18

Back then, the bust was shiny
reddish brown.
Now it looks totally different.

What colour is it now?

- ⬤ green
- ⬤ red
- ⬤ brown
- ⬤ black
- ⬤ blue
- ⬤ yellow

This Triton is a water-man, a friend of Neptune, god of the sea.
He sits on water and he blows water. He's as happy as can be!

Can you find the spot where the water came pouring out? ......fishhead......

Did you know that some people have a second toe that's longer than their big toe, just like this Triton?
That's something to be proud of, because it's supposed to be one of the classic signs of beauty.

Tulip vase

Delftware
1690

I've often dreamt about this:
a pretty vase full of tulips.

Here's a surprise for you:
a do-it-yourself kit! Make your own vase,
and impress your friends.

I'll tell you how to do it:

1. Remove the stickers and paste
   them on the next page.

2. Stack the parts – from large to small –
   on top of each other,
   and put the last piece on the very top.

3. Fill the spouts with water.

4. Now draw an imaginary flower in each spout.

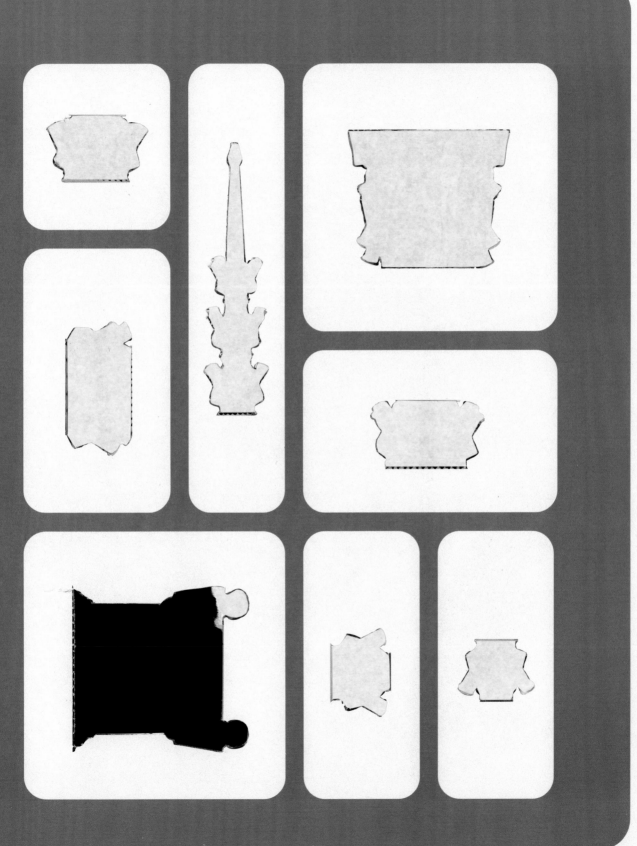

Noons Wijt:

Hendrick Avercamp

Winter landscape with ice skaters

1609

*I draw and paint landscapes and stories,
but the painter Hendrick Avercamp always
chooses the same subject. He's mad about fun
on the ice. There's so much to see in this painting,
it's like a picture riddle!*

26

On the dotted lines, write
down the spot where you
found each of these scenes:

1	**Girl pushes her brother**	A7	
2	**Skates for rent!**	......	
3	**Injuries during ice hockey**	B8.	
4	**No peeing here!**	......	
5	**17th-century graffiti**	......	
6	**Pants down**	......	
7	**Skirt up**	......	
8	**Fetching water**	......	

Willem Heda

Still life with gilt goblet

1635

This is a painting by Willem Heda.
Isn't this a tasty work of art?
In fact, it's so realistic that it's making me hungry.
I feel like slurping up an oyster. With a bit of pepper and lemon juice.
Why don't you join me? And now a good glass of wine.
Luckily the glass has bumps all over it,
that way it won't slip from my greasy fingers.
The table is laid with beautiful and costly objects.

Take your pencil and connect the things that go together. Find your way through the labyrinth.

What did you say? You don't like wine? Well, I'm certainly not about to drink water,
I don't want to get sick! In my day, the water was much too polluted to drink.

1. Oyster looking for pepper

2. Oyster looking for lemon juice

3. Wine jug looking for wine

4. Bread looking for beer

5. Knife looking for lemon

6. Pepper looking for salt

Frans Hals

Wedding portrait of
Isaac Massa en Beatrix van der Laan
1622

In this portrait the wealthy merchant Isaac and his wife Beatrix are sitting next to each other. They are newlyweds. Beatrix proudly shows us her wedding ring.

She is wearing the ring on her .... finger.

As a painter, I admire the way Frans Hals has painted their dark clothing. Positively brilliant!

Can you name three items of clothing that Isaac is wearing?

1 ....

2 ....

3 ....

See if you can copy Isaac's clothes with your pencil onto the left painting.

Isaac and Beatrix were no doubt familiar with the verse by the famous 17th-century poet Jacob Cats. It goes like this:

The ivy embraces the tree
With such a sturdy bond
Just as a lover does
With a lady on his arm.

Do you get it?
Just as the ivy found the tree, Isaac has also found Beatrix.

Rembrandt

Self-portrait

1628

Now we're standing face to face.
You're looking at me and I'm looking at you.
I can see you better than you can see me.

Why is that?

· ·

32

I've always enjoyed trying out all sorts of new things while I'm painting.
Here I used the other end of my brush to scratch lines in the paint while
it was still wet. If you look closely at my hair, you can see the effect.

Can you use the stickers
to tidy my hair?

Which words would you use
to describe my self-portrait?

○ **comical**   ○ **sad**

○ **mysterious**   ○ **happy**

○ **sleepy**   ○ **proud**

○ **serious**   ○ ....

Rembrandt-hair sticker page

Paste these stickers on the next page!

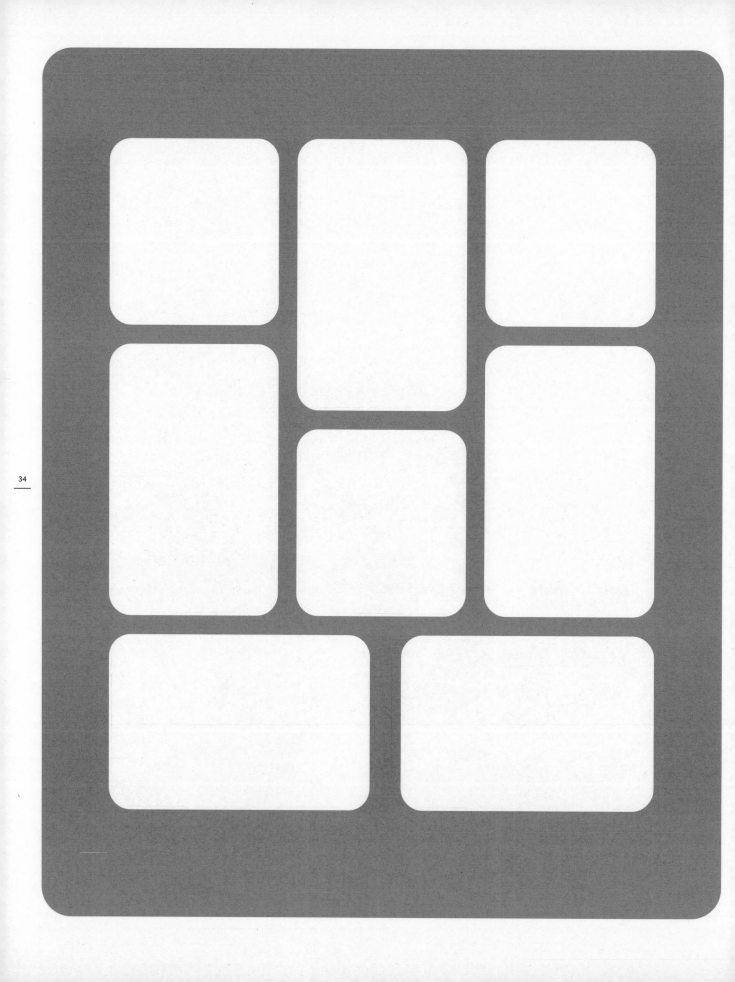

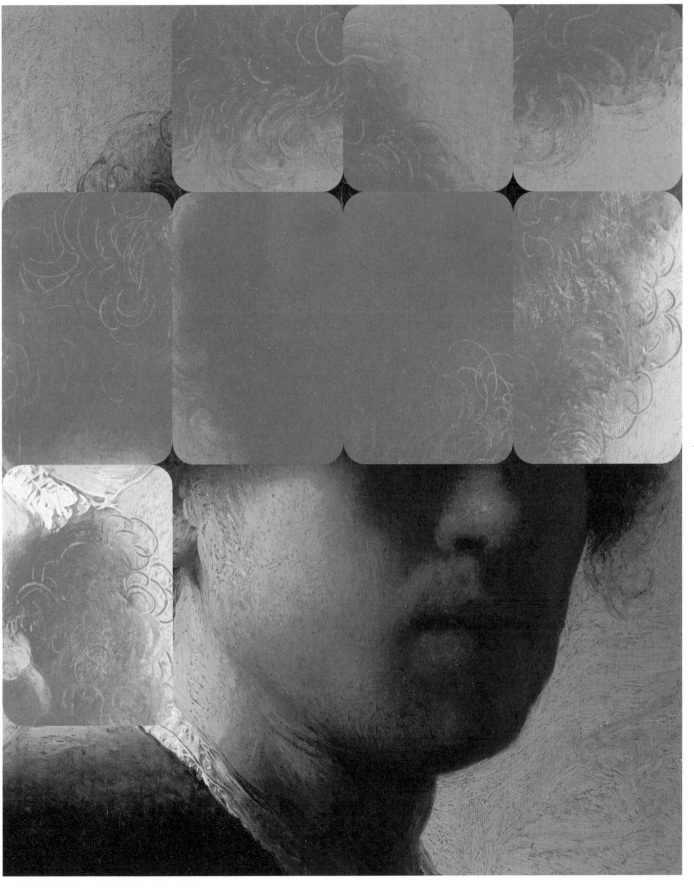

Rembrandt

Maria Trip

1639

There she stands, self-confidently: Maria Trip, a young woman of about twenty.
She came from a very wealthy family. You can tell that just by looking at her.
Everything she's wearing is expensive, exclusive and, of course, fashionable.
Apparently she's very fond of pearls.

What are pearls anyway?
Put an 'x' next to the correct answer:

○ **precious stones**

○ **globules of mother-of-pearl made by an oyster**

○ **shiny nuts that grow on pearl trees**

36

What do you see where? Take a good look.

1 Draw the pearls   **2 Draw the white lace**   **3 Draw the black lace**

Maria has a fan in her left hand. An umbrella would be of more use to her in Amsterdam,
but of course an exotic fan like this one is much more interesting!

4 Draw the gold brocade and the sections embroidered with gold thread

5 Draw her diamond brooch

6 Draw a circle where you think her navel is

Rembrandt

The Jewish bride
1665

*Some things are
private, even secret.
But as long as you're here,
take a really good look.*

*Don't forget to close the
door quietly behind you.*

In my earlier work I painted everything as precisely as possible: elegant ladies and gentlemen with gleaming pearls, huge collars and fine lace. Later I became more interested in emotions, and that's when I started painting more freely. You can see the difference in this painting. I paint not only with brushes, but with the other end of my paintbrush and my palette knife as well.

Where can you see that I've used my palette knife? Put 'x's' next to the correct answers:

- ○ in the eyes
- ○ in the sleeve
- ○ in the dress
- ○ in the woman's hair
- ○ in the hat

This painting is all about the quiet, loving relationship between two people. That's why I've used warm colours.

Can you name four of those colours?

1 ....   2 ....

3 ....   4 ....

That one's a bit tricky, isn't it? Sometimes painting is easier than writing!

And yet I thought long and hard about the colours. Suppose the woman had worn her blue dress. Do you think that would have changed the mood of the painting?

How would it have been different?

· ·

· ·

And finally, here's one to ponder:
are there two of them or three of them?

Did you know that the famous painter Vincent van Gogh also saw this painting?
He visited the Rijksmuseum in 1885.
Vincent said to a friend that he would give ten years of his life to be allowed
to sit in front of the painting for two weeks, with nothing but bread and water.

He called in an 'intimate and infinitely sympathetic' painting.
Of course, I felt very flattered by his comment.

Johannes Vermeer

The kitchen maid
1658-1660

*This painting by Johannes Vermeer is very famous.
And with good reason! Vermeer is at his best when he's
painting people and objects from his own surroundings.
Here we see a servant girl pouring milk. That's why
they also call her 'the milkmaid'.
The painting looks simple, but if you look closely,
you can see all kinds of detail.*

*The kitchen maid is making porridge with bread and milk.
She's concentrating very hard, so as not to spill a drop.
To be on the safe side, she's put on a clean blue apron and rolled up her sleeves.*

How can you tell that she usually wears long sleeves?

. . . .

*The bread is in the basket and on the table, but no doubt there's
more bread in the basket hanging on the wall.*

Why do you think the basket is hanging so high?

. . . .

Next to the basket hangs a brass bucket. The maid took the bucket with her when she went to the market to buy fish.
The blue jug is full of foaming beer. There is a footstove on the floor. A footstove is a kind of personal fireplace.
The maid could use it to warm her cold feet.

Connect the dots and colour in the maid.

Jan Steen

The merry family

1668

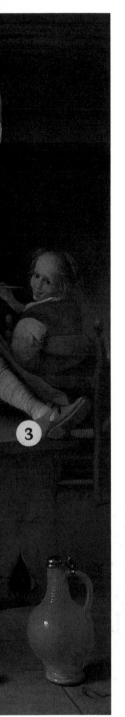

My colleague Jan Steen made a great many paintings. He was a phenomenal storyteller, and he often portrayed his own family life in lively scenes. Imagine what it would be like to have these people as your neighbours! You might find reason to complain about them.

Can you write down a list of complaints?

1 ....

2 ....

3 ....

4 ....

5 ....

I doubt if Jan Steen himself considered this an ideal household, for the message in the note on the mantelpiece is clearly a warning. The note reads: 'As the Old Sing, so the Young Twitter'.

Do you have any idea what the warning means?

. . . .

. . . .

In this painting, you can see Jan Steen himself playing the bagpipes. His wife Grietje van Goyen has the baby on her lap, grandmother is singing a song and grandfather is singing a duet with the dog.

Rembrandt

The Night Watch
1642

Here we are, then, standing in front of my most famous painting, 'The Night Watch'.

That's what everyone calls this painting, but what I painted wasn't a night watch at all If you people hadn't let the painting get so dirty, it probably wouldn't have been given such a 'dark' name. Luckily, the painting was thoroughly cleaned not too long ago, so now it looks the way it did when I painted it.

What you see here is a portrait of some Amsterdam militiamen. It was the job of the militiamen to defend the city. My painting is different from all the others: just look at the painting on the other side of the room, by my colleague Frans Hals:

*My men aren't posing. I've painted them in motion. There's an enormous
racket going on: I hear drums, people are all talking at once,
the dog is barking, there's even the sound of a rifle shot.*

1 Which rifleman is loading his gun?

. . . .

2 Where is a shot being fired?

. . . .

3 Where is the gunpowder being blown away?

. . . .

In the midst of this chaos, the captain takes charge and gives the order to march.

4 How can you tell that the
captain is giving the order?

. . . . and . . . .

*The light is coming from the top left.
You can tell by the shadow.*

Circle the shadow of the hand
on the lieutenant's suit.

The light also catches the girl, in her beautiful clothes.
You can see a chicken and a gun hanging from the belt
around her waist. Did you know that in the 17th century
a gun was called a 'clawer'? That's why I painted
the claws of a chicken here.

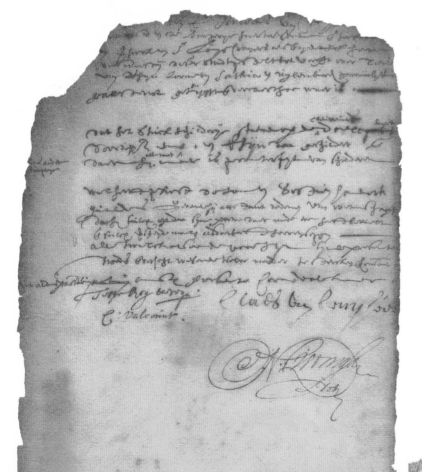

I have painted this painting. Yet I have
no idea how much it's worth. I've heard
stories about millions of euros.

In 1642 I was paid 1600 guilders
- which was a lot of money back
then - by the 16 riflemen who
commissioned the portrait.
Two more riflemen paid later.
← Here you can see the bill
    I sent them for my painting.

If you run your finger over the painting on this page, you can feel which riflemen didn't pay to have me paint them.

They've given the painting a fantastic spot here in the Rijksmuseum.
It's a shame people used to be so careless. Almost three hundred years ago three sections
along the edge were cut off, because the painting didn't fit in the room at the town hall.
Didn't they have any bigger rooms?

Rembrandt

Self-portrait

1661

Here I am again. I've done another painting of myself, but I'm a bit older here.

Can you figure out how old I am?

(I was born in 1606)

. . . .

Do you think I look pretty good for my age?

. . . .

Can you figure out how old the painting is now?

. . . .

Do you think the paint on the canvas is still

in good condition? . . . .

If you want to see this painting, walk back to the room where we saw 'The Jewish bride'.

I really enjoyed walking through the Rijksmuseum with you.
You'd be doing me a favour if you took the time to tell me what you thought of our little tour.
Would you write something about yourself, too? You can use the reply card on the back flap of this book.
Or you can send me an email. Go to: www.Rijksmuseum.nl/Rembrandt

I look forward to hearing from you!

Do you enjoy painting?
Then I have a couple of tips for you,
on how to make a Rembrandt of your own!

Take a sheet of paper or a piece
of real painter's linen.

Lay the paint on thicker rather than thinner.

You can take the blunt end of your
brush to use it to draw in the wet paint.

Use brushes, a palette knife or a trowel.

Don't make things too clear,
give people a chance to use their imagination.

Don't give the painting a name.
Let people think up a title of their own.

Answers by page number

p. 7
Europe	→	crown
Africa	→	sunbonnet
Asia	→	turban
America	→	feather headdress

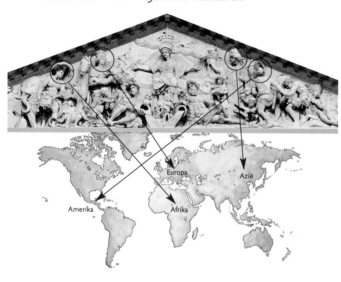

p. 8
- There's one man who doesn't have a moustache.
- There are two women in the painting.
- The glasses used during the feast:

p. 9
- The drummer has his serviette on his lap, which is a good thing because he eats with his hands.
- I count 5 knives in this painting.
- In the captain's shiny breastplate you can see a couple of riflemen who are sitting next to him at the table. The breastplate is almost like a mirror.

p. 11

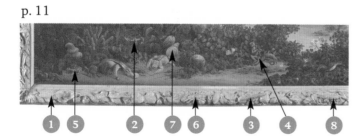

p. 17
8 o'clock	C		1 o'clock	F
9 o'clock	H		2 o'clock	G
10 o'clock	A		3 o'clock	I
11 o'clock	E		4 o'clock	D
12 o'clock	H		5 o'clock	E

p. 18
- I see the colours green, brown, red and black.
- The water was coming out of the head of the fish and the large shell he's sitting on.

p. 26
1	A7		8	A2-3 and B3
2	B4		9	B9
3	B8		10	A10
4	B-C6		11	A1
5	B2 and B11		12	B7
6	B2		13	C8
7	A3		14	A9

p. 31
- She's wearing the ring on her index finger.
- For the clothes, you can choose from: trousers, stockings, coat, ribbons, shoes and hat.

p. 32 Because I've painted my eyes and my mouth in shadow, I seem to be hiding.

p. 36 Pearls are globules of mother-of-pearl made by an oyster.

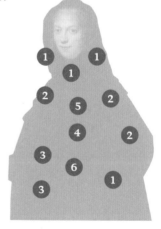

1	The pearls	4	The gold brocade
2	The white lace	5	The diamond brooch
3	The black lace	6	Her navel

Answers by page number

p. 40
- *I used my knife for the man's sleeve and the woman's dress.*
- *The warm colours are red, orange, yellow, ochre, brown and black.*
- *If I'd used other colours, the painting would have been much less intimate.*

p. 41
- *No one knows whether there are two of them or three. We see two people, but the woman may be pregnant, and then there are three of them. But some things are meant to be kept private.*

p. 42
- *Her arms aren't tanned, which means that she usually wears long sleeves.*
- *The bread is hung so high to keep it out of the reach of children and mice.*

p. 45
1. *Children aren't allowed to smoke.*
2. *Drunken men sing too loudly.*
3. *No shoes allowed on the sofa.*
4. *Children aren't supposed to drink wine.*
5. *Plates don't belong on the floor.*
- *The note means: If adults set a bad example, the children will imitate them.*

p. 47

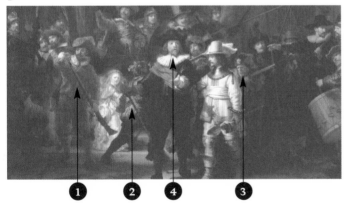

1 *The man in red, to the left of the captain, is loading his rifle.*
2 *The man who fired the shot is standing between the girl and the captain.*
3 *The man to the right of the lieutenant is blowing away the gunpowder.*
4 *The captain is the one giving the order, because he is speaking - his mouth is open - and he is giving the sign to start marching.*

p. 48 *The lion is embroidered on the edge of the jacket.*

p. 50
- *I'm 55 years old in the painting*
- *For those days, I don't look bad.*
- *In 2004 the painting was 343 years old.*
- *The paint on the canvas is still in pretty good shape.*

Information

Rijksmuseum Amsterdam
Address for visitors:
Jan Luijkenstraat 1
Postal address:
Postbus 74888
1070 DN Amsterdam
Latest information:
T +31 20 6747 000
F +31 20 6747 001
E info@rijksmuseum.nl
I   www.rijksmuseum.nl

Opening times
The Rijksmuseum is open daily
from 9 am to 18 pm,
closed on1 January.

How to get there
Tram 2 + 5 (Hobbemastraat stop)
Tram 6, 7 + 10 (Spiegelgracht stop)
The Rijksmuseum is free of charge
for visitors under 19 years of age.

Photography
Photography - without flash and tripod -
is permitted.

Mobile phones
It is not allowed to use your mobile phone.

Text
This guide was written by the Department of Education
& Information: Petra Kana-Devilee en Robert Uterwijk.

Translation
Barbara Fasting, and Overtaal BV, Utrecht.
The translation was made possible by a grant from the
Suman Fund.

Photography
Photography Department Rijksmuseum,
with the exception of: page 7 Royal Palace, Amsterdam,
photo: Jan Detwig; page 18 Frits Scholten; pag 48
Municipal Archives of Amsterdam.

Design
Studio Jas, Amsterdam

Illustrations:
Jorien Doorn, Bytes and Brushes

Floor plan
Irma Boom Office, Amsterdam

Printing
Drukkerij Ando - Calff & Meischke, Amsterdam

ISBN 90 400 8776 8
NUR 646

For more information on the activities of Waanders
Publishers and the Rijksmuseum, please visit
www.Rijksmuseum.nl and www.waanders.nl

WITH THANKS TO

PHILIPS

Sponsor LOTERIJ

Founder van Het *Nieuwe* Rijksmuseum